URBAN TRANSPORT IN ASEAN

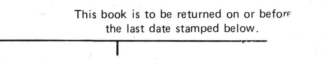
by

V. Setty Pendakur

with research assistance from
Ravi Pendakur

Research Notes and Discussions Paper No. 43
INSTITUTE OF SOUTHEAST ASIAN STUDIES
ASEAN Economic Research Unit
1984

Published by
Institute of Southeast Asian Studies
Heng Mui Keng Terrace
Pasir Panjang
Singapore 0511

ISSN 0129-8828
ISBN 9971-902-78-8

CONTENTS

ACKNOWLEDGEMENT

The encouragement by Professor K. S. Sandhu to pursue this topic is deeply appreciated. The author's tenure as a resident scholar at ISEAS provided the necessary opportunity to complete the paper, and this opportunity is gratefully acknowledged. Finally, thanks are due to Mrs Christina Goh for making the author's tenure at the Institute pleasant, easy and efficient.

V. Setty Pendakur

I

INTRODUCTION

ASEAN Cities and Urban Transport

Developing countries are urbanizing at a very rapid rate. Between 1980 and the year 2000, the urban areas of developing countries could add almost one billion people to their already large populations. The size and scale of such projected growth offer serious challenges to urban planners in the context of increasing demand for urban services, especially when available resources are not growing at the same rate.

The number of very large cities is also increasing rapidly. In 1950, only one city in the developing countries had a population of more than five million. By the end of the century, some forty cities are expected to be at or above the five million level (Linn 1983). Such a pace of urban growth poses unprecedented challenges to planners, particularly in the areas of housing, employment, and transport. In this context, the efficient and equitable delivery of urban services becomes a central issue. While it is important to accommodate both growth and modernization, it should not become burdensome or inequitable to large sections of the urban population, particularly the poor.

Concurrent with the explosion in human population over the past three decades in Southeast Asia, there has been a more striking explosion in the automobile population. For, although the degree of motorization indicated by automobile ownership rates is low compared to the industrialized countries, the ownership of automobiles has been increasing at a markedly high rate. The most remarkable feature of these two simultaneous explosions is that both are concentrated in the major metropolitan areas.

The populations of such metropolitan areas as Jakarta, Manila, and Bangkok (each in excess of five million) dwarf the

1

populations of other cities in the region. In income, socio-economic activity and production, these cities are even more important than their populations indicate. For example, the estimated value of goods and services (or gross national product) produced in Manila exceeds the total GNP of several other Asian countries (World Bank 1982).

The role played by transport in providing efficient mobility and accessibility to keep the urban economy functioning is of prime importance. The efficiency of the urban transport system is a major indicator of the productivity and livability of a city (World Bank 1975). The physical structure of a city, its size and density, its standard of living and character are all dependent to a large degree upon the nature and quality of the urban transport system. The vitality and the efficiency of the urban transport system provided in a city affects the way in which the city and its citizens function.

Improvements to and building of new infrastructure have been recognized to be prerequisites to successful planning. Physical infrastructure has consumed about 20-50% of annual public expenditures in many countries. Transport's pivotal role in moving increasing numbers of people and quantity of goods has resulted in some countries devoting 15-20% of their annual GDP (gross domestic product) to this sector (World Bank 1972). The South East Asian Regional Transport survey indicated that the transport sector in each of the member countries of the Association of Southeast Asian Nations (ASEAN) would require 20-30% of the national GDP for a decade or more (Little et al. 1972).

During 1965-80, all the large urban areas of the ASEAN countries conducted major urban transportation studies covering future growth patterns and the projected transport needs. Currently, some cities are building new systems (such as the Light Rapid Transit or LRT in Manila) and others are in the process of doing so (the Mass Rapid Transit or MRT in Singapore and Bangkok). These new systems in the five ASEAN capital cities alone are expected to cost US$5-8 billion, and are to be built during the 1980-95 period.

The urban transport systems in the ASEAN countries reflect a unique vitality and variety, providing almost demand responsive services. They consist of diverse public-vehicle systems ranging from the **becak**, **bemo**, jeepney, minibus and the more common stage-bus to private systems such as cars, motor-cycles, company buses and contract vehicles. The secondary transport system (other than private transport and the stage-bus) operates in a fiercely competitive private enterprise environment. Its vitality and transport role have been studied by several researchers (Grava 1972 and 1978; Rimmer 1982; Roth 1977 and 1982; Pendakur 1976, and 1981a; Rimmer and Dick 1980) in the past decade. These studies suggest that the secondary transport system is vital to the efficient functioning of cities and it has significant socio-economic linkages to and multipliers in the urban economy. For example, it was estimated that in 1975, about 10% of the labour force of Manila was directly or indirectly involved in the provision of jeepney services (World Bank 1976). Another study indicated that the livelihood of nearly 8% of the total population of Manila was directly related to the jeepneys (Pendakur 1976). Allowing for biases in these estimates, these studies are clearly indicative of the importance of the secondary transport systems.

New urban transport systems requiring large investments are being built in ASEAN cities. The consequent modernization is being superimposed on a secondary transport system which has been praised as a vital service and, at the same time, blamed as inefficient, archaic, backward, and wasteful. There are obviously some inefficiencies of scale and size. However, the demand responsive nature, private enterprise and profitability character, accessibility and manoeuvrability, and the socio-economic multipliers may outweigh the inefficiencies and disadvantages.

Purpose and Scope of the Study

This study assumes that urbanization will continue at a rapid pace in ASEAN commensurate with forecasts made by other researchers (U.N. Secretariat 1980; Salih 1981). It is further assumed that the ASEAN capital cities will continue to grow at a rapid rate and remain primate in their role. This study describes, discusses and analyses the urban transport phenomena in this context.

No original data were collected for this study alone although the author's work in ASEAN as a scholar and professional consultant to various international agencies has assisted in data collection. The urban areas were chosen not only because they are important but also because data were available. The data sets have been updated to the most recent transportation studies.

The study focuses on the urban transport sector in the context of urbanization and growth. It describes existing systems and discusses the policy implications of modernization. The emphasis is on the range of vehicles and persons within the secondary transport system.

3

As the data were drawn from a number of sources and then reconciled for tabulation, the component data elements for all cities are not always for the same year. However, it is accurate and adequate enough for broad policy analysis. Finally, this study suggests further research efforts to better understand tne role of urban transport in general, and secondary transport in particular, in ASEAN.

THE URBAN CONTEXT

Background

The countries of ASEAN are essentially middle-income economies among the developing countries (World Bank 1982). Their GNP, per capita income and general level of well-being are much better than many other countries of Asia. With the exception of Singapore, they are middle-sized countries in terms of both population and land area. Data presented in Table 1 show that their economies have been growing at a moderately high rate during the past decade.

The period 1950-80 has been one of high population growth rates combined with large-scale urbanization. Urbanization in ASEAN is occurring under very different circumstances compared to the industrialized countries. Some of the characteristics are:

1. rapid population growth;

2. strictly controlled international immigration and barriers to immigration (unlike the European Economic Community);

3. dominance of a very small number of cities;

4. decreasing and/or stable costs of transport and communications up to 1975, and geometric increases in those costs since then;

5. transport costs becoming a heavy burden on balance of payments since 1975.

During the period of rapid urbanization in Europe, the

TABLE 1

Population and Urbanization in ASEAN

ASEAN COUNTRY	Country Data					Largest City/Metropolis *					Sources
	1980 GNP (per capita: US$)	Population in Millions		Annual Growth Rate 1970-80 (%)	Percent Urban	ASEAN PRIMATE CITIES	Population in Millions		Population as a % of Country		World Bank 1982. U.N. Secretariat 1980.
		Estimates						Estimates			
		1980	2000		1980	2000		1980	2000	1980	2000	
INDONESIA	430	146.6	216	2.3%	20	31	JAKARTA	6.5	16.9	4.4	7.8	* For the purposes of this paper, Jakarta means Jakarta Metropolitan DKI Area as in 1980.
MALAYSIA	1620	13.9	21	2.4%	29	45	KUALA LUMPUR	1.0	2.1	7.2	10	Kuala Lumpur Federal Territory including Petaling Jaya as in 1980.
PHILIPPINES	690	49.0	77	2.7%	36	51	MANILA	5.9	12.7	12	16.5	Metro Manila as in 1980.
SINGAPORE	4430	2.4	3	1.5%	100	100	SINGAPORE	2.4	3.0	100	100	Singapore as in Republic of Singapore.
THAILAND	670	47	68	2.5%	14	27	BANGKOK	5.3	11.0	11.3	16.2	Bangkok means Bangkok-Thonburi Metropolitan Area as in 1980.

national population growth rates were typically low, at about 0.5% per year. In constrast, the growth rates in the ASEAN countries have been typically in the order of 2 to 3% per year (Beier et al. 1975; World Bank 1982). These high rates of population growth have resulted from larger absolute population movements to cities as well as natural increases within the cities. The consequent pressure to absorb large numbers of people through the provision of employment and services has resulted in a different type of urbanization requiring different policy responses. These growth rates are expected to remain relatively high, at least for the next two decades.

Data shown in Table 1 indicate that the growth rates in the ASEAN countries, with the exception of Singapore, will remain at about 2% per annum. The combined population of the five countries is expected to increase from 259 million in 1980 to 385 million in the year 2000 (Table 1). Their urban population will increase even more rapidly than the absolute growth. Thailand's urban population, which was a mere 14% of its total in 1980, is expected to increase to 27% in the year 2000; Indonesia's from 20 to 31%; Malaysia's from 29 to 45%; and the Philippines' from 36 to 51%. This means that the pressure on the cities to provide more jobs, housing, and services will continue to increase.

Several dimensions of ASEAN urbanization are important in the context of the increasing demand for urban services, particularly housing and transport. Some of the more important aspects are:

1. the levels of urbanization are low compared to the industrialized countries, but the rate of urbanization is quite high;

2. Malaysia and the Philippines show similar levels and rates of urbanization, whereas Indonesia and Thailand form another group;

3. urban growth rates are expected to decrease but yet remain substantially higher than the rural growth rates (Table 1).

There are several other important characteristics of urbanization in ASEAN. Urban unemployment rates are substantially higher than those in rural areas. There is also substantial underemployment except in Singapore.

A significant proportion of the urban population live in slums and squatter areas. It was estimated that 26% of the population of Jakarta (1972) lived in slums and squatter settlements*, as did 27% in Bandung (1972), 30% in Bangkok (1976), 35% in Kuala Lumpur (1973) and 35% in Manila (1972) (Linn 1983; Salih 1981). The provision of urban services, particularly their level and cost, must take into serious consideration the level of poverty and unemployment. This is particularly important in relation to urban transport because mobility is necessary for productive activity; yet mobility costs money. The poor have more time than money. They require transport to search for employment. Also, their time is not easily translated into money. Therefore, they require inexpensive transport.

The ASEAN capital cities are dominant demographic, economic, political, and social centres. They are primate cities dominating the national urban system. This domination pervades economic, social, and political activity. The second-level cities of ASEAN are dwarfed by the primate cities both in population size and economic power. Furthermore, all of these cities will grow in importance and size by the year 2000 (Table 1).

Selected Urban Areas of ASEAN

The urban areas included in this study are shown in Table 2. They were selected on the basis of their size, their status in the heirarchy of the national urban system, the availability of data, the nature of secondary transport available, and the reliability of data. All the ASEAN primate/capital cities are included, but Singapore is discussed only briefly because it is an exception in many respects. Second-tier cities in which secondary transport systems play a significant role have also been included as they were thought necessary to provide a contrast to the very large metropolitan primate cities. Thus, Surabaya, Bandung, and Chiang Mai were added to the list.

---

*   Slum/squatter settlements are as defined by the United Nations and adopted by the International Labour Organization. Data shown here are the numbers of slum/ squatter households as a percentage of total households in the metropolitan area, and are adapted from Salih 1981 and Lin 1983.

8

TABLE 2

Population, Density and Income in Selected Urban Areas

ASEAN City	City Size (km²)	Population ('000)	Density Persons/km²	Per Capita Income/Year (US$)	Population Projection AD 2000 ('000)	Sources
Bandung, INDONESIA	81[a]	1,836[b] (1980)	22,700	134[a] (1975)	4,126[b]	a. Soegijoko 1979. b. Salih 1981.
Jakarta, INDONESIA	650[a]	6,500[b] (1980)	10,000	325[c] (1971)	16,900[b]	a. Wheel Extended 1979. b. Salih 1981. c. Owen 1973.
Surabaya, INDONESIA	290[a]	2,273[b] (1980)	7,480	212[a] (1974)	5,038[b]	a. Fouracre & Maunder 1978. b. Salih 1981.
Kuala Lumpur, MALAYSIA	243[a]	1,031[b] (1980)	4,240	660[c] (1970)	1,500[d]	a. Author's data files. b. Fouracre & Maunder 1982. c. Zahavi 1976. d. Salih 1981.
Manila, PHILIPPINES	636[a]	5,900[b] (1980)	9,280	436[d] (1975)	12,900[c]	a. Ocampo 1982[b]. b. Republic of Philippines 1982. c. Salih 1981. d. Case and Latchford 1981.
Bangkok-Thonburo, THAILAND	1,570[a]	5,330[a] (1981)	3,400	525[b] (1970)	11,000[c]	a. JICA 1982. b. Zahavi 1976. c. Salih 1981.
Chiang Mai, THAILAND	18[a]	110[a] (1978)	6,100	*	142[b]	a. Bandhachat 1979. b. Chivakul 1982.

* Data not available.

Bandung

Bandung is the capital of West Java and the third largest city in Indonesia next only to Jakarta and Surabaya. It is an established centre of higher learning as well as a regional manufacturing centre. The major industries are pharmaceuticals and textiles. The city is located in a fertile valley and is endowed with a moderate and pleasant climate. It is well connected by a variety of transportation routes and modes to other Indonesian cities.

The population of Bandung was approximately 1 million in 1960. It was estimated to be 1.8 million in 1980. The growth rate was about 2.5% per annum during the sixties and was substantially higher during the following decade. It is estimated that by the year 2000, Bandung will have 4.1 million people (U.N. Secretariat 1980).

Bandung is a high-density city with 22,700 persons per km^2 (Table 2). Jobs are heavily concentrated in the service sector -- 44% in 1982. The job opportunities are expected to continue to grow, providing a base for population growth. The dependency ratio (employment to total population) is quite low at 3.7 (including informal sector jobs) (Soegijiko 1979).

A large portion of Bandung's population cannot afford satisfactory housing and does not have adequate infrastructure services. In 1972, 27% of the city's population lived in slums and squatter settlements (Linn 1983).

Bandung has an inadequate urban transport system. Standard buses are not allowed to operate within the city but ply only the inter-city routes. Motorized public transport consists of minibuses and microbuses. The **becak** (bicycle rickshaw) is the backbone of the public transport system.

Jakarta

Jakarta is the largest city in Southeast Asia and, based on current growth trends, will likely remain so. The city grew from 2.9 million in 1961 to 4.6 million in 1971 (about 58%). The 1980 population was 6.5 million, and it is expected to grow to 16.9 million by the year 2000 (Table 2). Jakarta is a primate city dominating all other urban areas and their economic activities. It has three times the population of the second largest city, Surabaya.

Depending upon the method of estimation (and source),

between 30 and 50% of the total Jakarta Metropolitan Area (DKI) is urbanized. The Jakarta Metropolitan Area Transportation Study (JMATS) study estimated that approximately half of the DKI area had some form of urban development. Nearly a third (32%) of the urban land was for squatter-type residential use (Republic of Indonesia 1975).

The World Bank, in its **Second Urban Development Project Appraisal Report,** estimated that only 170 km^2 of the total DKI area was urbanized (**Wheel Extended,** 1979a). The gross population density for the DKI area in 1980 was 10,000 persons/km^2 (Table 2). However, if only the urbanized area was considered, the density would be 38,235 persons/km^2.

Jakarta could be considered a relatively amorphous urban area. It possesses no single strong central business district but has a number of areas with concentrated economic activity. Mixed within the residential areas are the local **pasar** in which a wide variety of local goods and services can be obtained (**Wheel Extended,** 1979a). Per capita annual income was on the low side at US$325 in 1971 (Table 2). With only 4.4% of the country's population in 1980, Jakarta produced 9.5% of the national GNP.

A large section of Jakarta's population cannot afford satisfactory housing and the city does not have adequate infrastructure services. In 1972, 26% of the total households were living in slums and in squatter settlements (Salih 1981). More than 50% of Jakarta's population live in kampongs where densities can reach more than 100,000 persons/km^2. The physical conditions in most kampongs are barely above the slum level, lacking in drinking water, sanitation or other basic infrastructure (Republic of Indonesia 1982).

Jakarta's transportation system is not adequate for a fast growing metropolis. The public transport system consists of buses, minibuses and an insignificant commuter rail. Jakarta's transport modernization policy emphasizes the replacement of the low-technology secondary transport systems (**becak** and **jitney**) with a system of stage-buses and minibuses, and is considered a model for other Indonesian cities. The **jitneys** have been relegated to a subordinate connecting (link trip) role and the **becaks** are being abolished.

Surabaya

Surabaya is the second largest city in Indonesia and had a population of 2.3 million in 1980. It covers an area of 290 km^2, and has an overall density of 7,840 persons/km^2 (Table 2).

However, the built-up area is only 70 km^2 with a density of 26,500 persons/km^2 (Fouracre and Maunder 1978). Its population is expected to reach five million by the year 2000 (Table 2).

Surabaya is strategically located in East Java and is the regional centre for transport (ports), communications, and industry. It has grown rapidly from a population of only 679,000 in 1950 to 1.47 million in 1970.

The per capita annual income of residents in Surabaya was lower than that of the people in Jakarta but comparable to those in other Indonesian cities, at US$212 in 1974. As in Jakarta, over 50% of the city's population live in kampongs where densities can be as high as 100,000 persons/km^2. Infrastructure services are either not available, or of very low quality. The kampongs are serviced by narrow alleys, with no proper roads, and can only be reached on foot, by motor-cycle, bicycle or **becak** (Fouracre and Maunder 1978).

Kuala Lumpur (KL)

Kuala Lumpur, the Federal Capital of Malaysia, was designated a Federal Territory in 1974 and comes under the direct control of the Federal Government. The urban area (Federal Territory) is 243 km^2 and includes Petaling Jaya. Initially a trading centre in Selangor state, KL is now the government, commercial and financial centre of the country.

At the time of independence in 1957, the population of KL's urban area was 380,000 including those living in the new town of Petaling Jaya about 10 km west of the city. By 1973, the population had increased to 860,000 and was estimated at 1.03 million in 1978. The annual population growth rate was 3.7% during the sixties and was estimated at 6% during the seventies. It is expected to grow at an annual rate of 4% and reach 1.5 million by the year 2000 (Table 2). With only 4,240 persons/km^2, KL was a lower density urban environment compared to other ASEAN cities. The per capita annual income was, however, the highest among all the cities shown in Table 2.

Jobs are heavily concentrated in the administrative and services sectors (about 40%), which is typical for a national capital, and in manufacturing (about 20%). The corresponding figures for Peninsular Malaysia are only about 20% and 10% respectively. As jobs in these sectors increase more rapidly than in others, it is unlikely that the population growth rates can be checked.

A large proportion of KL's population cannot afford satisfactory housing and does not have access to adequate infrastructure services. A large proportion of the population squat on public and private land as do a similarly high proportion of small businesses. It was estimated that 35% of all households in 1973 lived in slums or in squatter settlements (Salih, 1981). An inadequate public transport system severely restricts the poor from proper access to employment opportunities.

Manila

Manila is also called the National Capital Region. It is composed of four cities and 13 municipalities and was constituted in November 1975 by a Presidential Decree. Manila, which covers less than 0.5% of the land area, contains 41% of the country's total population.

The city is characterized by an over-concentration of economic, social and political enterprises and is the seat of a highly centralized government. It is also the centre for commerce, education, and industry. About 60% of the country's non-agricultural labour force is employed here and about 90% of the internal revenue collections for the entire country are from this source. Manila has had very high rates of population growth because of both natural increases and migration. It grew from 2.5 million in 1960 to 3.9 million in 1970, and to 5.9 million in 1980 (Republic of the Philippines 1982b; and Table 2).

Manila is the largest single urban area in the Philippines. It is a primate city overwhelming other urban areas in population size and commerce. Its population is eight times that of the second largest city, Davao, and ten times that of the third largest city, Cebu. It produces approximately one-third of the national GNP, which accounts for the fact that 50% of the secondary industry and all of the tertiary activities are located there. Its population increases by about 4 million per year, with an average household size of 5.5. Manila is the largest educational centre in the country with 1.8 million students (Dent 1981).

It was estimated that 35% of Manila's population in 1972 were living in slums and squatter settlements (Grimes 1976). However, the car ownership and motorization rates are increasing very rapidly. The number of private cars increased by 60% during 1975-80 whereas the number of buses plummeted from 4,000 to 2,000 during the same period. There are one million motor vehicles registered in the Philippines, of which 50% are in Manila (Dent

13

1981). The annual rate of increase is in the order of 9-10%.

Bangkok

Bangkok, the 200-year-old capital of Thailand, is located in the central coastal region on a fertile alluvial plain along the lower Chao Phya river. The emergence of Bangkok as a primate city is due to the fact that since its establishment in 1782, attempts have been made to make it the centre of all things in Thailand - commerce, industry, government, education, and religion. Although its growth was hampered by World War II, it gained momentum during the 1960s primarily due to large public-sector investments. In 1971, Bangkok and Thonburi were merged to form the Bangkok Metropolitan area. It has grown rapidly from a population of 1.9 million in 1961, to 3.0 million in 1971 and to 5.3 million in 1981 (Virabalin and Prosith-rathasint 1982). Its population is estimated to reach 11.0 million by the year 2000 (Table 2).

Bangkok had a gross population density of 3,400 persons/km^2 (Table 2). This, on the surface, appears to be a low density Asian environment, but a large portion of the area is not urbanized. The most densely populated sections of Bangkok now have a density approaching 100,000 persons/km^2. Bangkok has continually had the highest percentage of Thailand's urban population. In 1971, it had 85% of the total urban population, which decreased to 76% in 1982. It dwarfs all other urban areas in size and economic activity. For example, in 1982 its population was 48 times the population of the second largest city, Chiang Mai.

A large portion of Bangkok's population does not have adequate housing or physical infrastructure services. It was estimated that in 1976, 30% of all households in Bangkok either were slum dwellers or lived in squatter settlements (Salih 1981).

The car population has grown at an average annual rate of 16% over the last fifteen years and the motor-cycle population at 34%. There is an acute shortage of public transport in Bangkok. Serious traffic congestion in central Bangkok is an everyday phenomenon.

Chiang Mai

Chiang Mai is the second largest city in Thailand, located 700 km northwest of Bangkok. It is the largest and the most modern city in northern Thailand. It has been growing over the past fifteen years at an annual rate of 2.4% (Suntaranont 1982).

Chiang Mai is a major communication centre, the principle employment centre of northern Thailand, a university city and a major tourist centre, as well as the main trading and business centre for the region. The population of Chiang Mai city in 1978 was 110,000 and is expected to grow to 142,000 by the turn of the century. The urban area had a population density of 6,100 persons/km^2 (Table 2).

The city is located on a plain with a mountain backdrop. The river runs through the eastern half of the city, making the transportation system somewhat distorted. The city is laid out in a combination of grid and radial streets. It is served by a public transport system essentially designed, managed, and operated by private operators and consists mainly of minibuses (**silors**) -- converted vans.

III

URBAN TRANSPORT SYSTEMS IN ASEAN

System Significance

The role played by urban transport in providing the mobility and accessibility to keep the urban economy functioning is of paramount importance and is multi-dimensional in nature. Its basic function is to provide efficient links between homes and jobs, and the users and producers of goods and services. It complements a large number of other urban public services because the level of accessibility and mobility determines to a considerable extent the efficiency of many other services (such as fire protection, waste disposal, drainage, education and health). The efficiency of the urban transport system is a substantial indicator of the productivity and livability of a city.

The physical structure of the city, its size and sprawl, its way of life and character, are all dependent upon the nature and quality of the transport system. The vitality, the universal availability and the cost of urban transport deeply affect the way in which the city and its citizens function. Because the transport system has such a primary impact on a city's extension, sprawl and population density, it also has a considerable effect on the cost of other urban services.

The urban transport sector is important in other ways as well. It provides employment for a significant, although varying proportion, of the urban population. In 1980, for example, 11% of the total labour force in Singapore was employed in the transportation sector (Chief Statistician 1983) and in Bangkok it was 6% (JICA 1982). It was estimated that 10% of the labour force in Manila in 1975 was directly or indirectly involved in the provision of jeepney services alone (1975 World Bank data; Linn 1983). In 1975 the jeepneys provided the livelihood for an estimated 350,000 persons in Manila (Pendakur 1976).

The construction and maintenance of urban transport systems place a considerable fiscal burden on the cities. It is not unusual for urban governments to spend 15-25% of their annual budgets on transport-related investments and operating activities (Linn 1983). Total rapid transit modernization (LRT/MRT) expenditures projected for ASEAN capitals for the 1980-90 period alone are expected to reach US$5-8 billion. The Southeast Asian Regional Transport survey indicated that the urban transport sector would require 10-15% of the national GDP for a decade or more (Little et al. 1972).

The rapid urbanization in ASEAN cities has had a tremendous impact on their transportation systems, particularly in the primate cities. The spatial expansion to accommodate the new populations in the new suburbs at considerable distance from the centre, with visible concentration of jobs in the central city, has compelled many people to travel long distances just for survival. For example, in small cities, virtually all destinations can be reached on foot, by bicycle, or **becak**, but the people in the large cities are compelled to use motorized transport. As a result, congestion and pollution have taken on much more serious and widespread proportions (Linn 1979).

The urban transport system, especially its public transport component, is particularly important to the urban poor as it provides them with easy access to jobs at affordable costs. The poor are obviously at the margin of subsistence and are particularly vulnerable to transport cost increases which disrupt and distort their incomes. This applies to them whether they are employees or in business carrying on formal/informal commercial and trading activities. Furthermore, the transport sector itself provides the urban poor with a considerable number of employment opportunities and these opportunities can be expanded or contracted depending upon the socio-economic goals of the urban transport policies. Thus, the level of service, the cost of expansion, and modernization are critically important to the urban poor.

Urbanization and motorization have occurred concurrently in ASEAN. Cities are becoming larger, more affluent and more motorized. There has been a phenomenal growth in personal motor vehicles (cars and motor-cycles) that visibly clutter and congest the streets of the ASEAN cities. For example, in Bangkok during the five-year period of 1976-81 alone, there was a 66% increase in the number of private cars and a 190% increase in motor-cycles (JICA 1982). During the same period in Singapore, even under conditions of restraint because of high user taxes, private cars increased by 19% and motor-cycles by 52% (Chief Statistician 1983). On the other hand, in Jakarta private cars increased by 28% and motor-cycles by 74%, and in Manila, private cars by 170%

17

(Republic of the Philippines 1982). During the same period, the human population in Bangkok increased by 30%, in Singapore by 11% and in Manila by 26%. Of the two population explosions, human beings and private motor-vehicles, the motor-vehicle population explosion has been larger, more significant and more pronounced. Of all the motor vehicles registered in 1981 in the Philippines (1.0 million), 50% were in Manila (Dent 1981) and 79% of all motor vehicles registered in 1981 in Thailand were in Bangkok (JICA 1982).

ASEAN cities are coping with as much automobile traffic as some of the most motorized cities of Canada and the United States but with far less roadways, a tremendous mixture of vehicles of different speeds and capacities, a mixture of motorized and non-motorized vehicles, the absence of MRT/LRT and generally very meagre resources. The efficiency of ASEAN cities and, therefore, the significance of urbanization to development will depend, to a large degree, on how the problems of mobility are resolved. A key factor will be the degree to which motorized transport, both private and public, can be controlled and contained equitably in the interest of a satisfactory total urban system.

System Structure and Ownership

Although private-vehicle ownership has grown in the ASEAN countries at a very high rate during the past two decades, a very large portion of the population is dependent upon public transport. The middle- and lower-income population will continue to walk, cycle and use available modes of public transport. In ASEAN, the mere ownership of a motor-cycle/scooter or a car signifies an upper-middle and upper-income class. However, the vast majority will continue to depend upon public transport as the only means of transport. Hence, the availability and cost of public transport is very significant to the lower-income urban residents.

ASEAN public transport systems display significant vitality and diversity because of the unique, decentralized and diverse vehicles, ownership patterns, competitive free enterprise and the innovative energies of owners and users. A large number of vehicles provide service and operate within the formal sector. Often, an equally large number operate within the informal sector. There is a great deal of innovation in providing an almost demand responsive service as individual units and enterprises respond to increasing and decreasing demand cycles with very little state interference. In spite of pressures from the state during the last two decades to consolidate and

18

centralize, the systems still retain a large degree of diversity and, therefore, vitality. In most ASEAN cities, the number of informal vehicles (illegal, pirate, without licence, etc.) are almost as many as the formal vehicles in the same categories. For example, in Manila in 1981, only 17,500 jeepneys were licensed to operate whereas it was estimated that there were nearly 35,000 jeepneys providing daily service (Republic of the Philippines 1982).

The traditional component of the public transport system, the bus (the stage-bus) still plays an important role. Both public and private systems co-exist in ASEAN. In general, the publicly owned and operated systems are financially loss incurring systems. The political control over operating policies (routes, frequency, and fares) appears to be the main reason for the large operating deficits. The Singapore Bus System (SBS) is government supported (the government is a minority shareholder) but privately owned. It is a very well-run profit-making enterprise. Private bus systems in Jakarta are profit-making despite the fact that they charge the same fare as the public (loss-making) system and have less desirable routes. In general, the private operators can be expected to respond quickly to changes in demand, be interested in cutting costs, and to have better control of revenues than the public sector (Roth 1980). In Manila, the privately owned systems operate with a profit whereas the publicly owned Metro Manila Transit Corporation (MMTC) is heavily subsidized. The Bangkok public transport system owned and operated by the Bangkok Mass Transit Authority (BMTA) requires very heavy annual subsidies whereas the minibuses operated by private owners are profit-making enterprises. However, some of the losses suffered by the public systems could be caused by political decisions especially where fares are kept at an artificially low level and the system is required to provide service to areas where there is less demand.

During the period 1945-75, the theory and practice in North America was that urban public transport was a public good and therefore must be publicly owned and supplied. The assumption underlying these notions was that there was no reason to have a profit motive for a basic-needs service. Therefore, during that period, most urban transport systems in North America and Europe were consolidated into single publicly owned and operated units. They were given a monopoly franchise and came under the direct political control of urban/regional/state governments. Recent history, particularly in the period 1975-80, indicates that these systems provide slow, costly and unprofitable service requiring vast amounts of annual operating subsidies. The run-away costs can be attributed partly to inflation in wages and fuel costs but mainly to political control of routes and fare structure, and operating philosophy.

19

System Structure and Fleet Size

ASEAN cities have a vast range of vehicle types supplementing the public bus. These secondary urban transport modes are the jeepney and tricycle (Manila), minibus and microbus (Kuala Lumpur, Jakarta, and Bangkok), **bemo** and **silor** (Bangkok and Jakarta), **becak**, trishaw and **samlor** (Bangkok, Kuala Lumpur, and Jakarta) and **helicak** (Surabaya and Bandung). All of these vehicles are smaller than a standard bus, are versatile, can travel along narrow roads and lanes, can provide door-to-door service in most instances, and reflect great variety and local innovation. They are either converted jeeps or vans, improved cab versions of a motor-cycle or a bicycle or just small buses or big vans. Their capacities can vary from only two seats (**becak**) to sixteen seats (jeepney). They provide individualized taxi service at very low cost, substantially cheaper than the traditional taxi and slightly more expensive than the bus. They are very popular modes of transport and reflect a wide range of energy efficiencies (Table 3).

The components of the secondary transport system are, in general, private-enterprise units operating under government regulatory umbrellas. These units are generally small, giving them flexibility in both operation and management. Often, the ownership and driving of the vehicles are shared by family members. Even though the number of vehicles and routes are regulated and franchised, the ownership, tenure and management systems are informal.

Some of the units belong to route associations (Malaysia), and transport co-operatives (Philippines). This formal structure has been imposed by the governments presumably in the interests of economies of scale. Although the formal structure was resisted in the beginning, they seem to be working well. However, a vast majority of these units continue to operate within the informal sector.

The individualistic nature of the enterprise and the diversity of ownership patterns have helped to maintain the competitive nature of the service. The secondary transport systems have hitherto avoided being pooled into monopoly systems as in Western countries. For example, in Manila in 1976, 19% of the jeepneys were owned by enterprises with only one unit, 10% with two-units, 7% with three-units, 6% with four-units, while 25% of the jeepneys belonged to enterprises owning 5-9 units, and 17% to those owning 10-14 units. This means that 65% of the jeepneys were in enterprises owning less than 10 units. However, if only the number of enterprises were considered, 55% of the enterprises had only one unit, 15% had two units, 7% had three units and 4% had four units. This means that 84% of the

TABLE 3

Secondary Urban Transport Modes

Transit Mode	Vehicle Description	Energy* Consumption (L/100 Pass/Km)	ASEAN Country	References
Jeepney Jitney Opelet	Converted Jeep (6-20 Passengers) Converted Sedan (6-8 Passengers)	0.8	Philippines Indonesia	Grava 1972 & 1980; Luna 1978; Walters 1979; Ocampo 1982 a&b; Republic of the Philippines 1982; Pendakur 1976 & 1981 a&b.
Microbus Minibus Queue bus	Small Bus or Converted Van or Jeep (6-14 Passengers)	0.8	Malaysia Thailand Indonesia	Dick 1981 a&b; Pendakur 1976, 1981 a&b & 1982; Fouracre & Maunder 1980; Rimmer & Dick 1980; Walters 1979; Jamieson McKay 1981; Metropolis 1976.
Helicak Bajaj	Motor-cycle Engine & Drive with 2 seats behind Driver	0.8	Indonesia	Fouracre & Maunder 1978.
Bemo Silor	Large Helicak (6-8 Passengers)	0.8	Indonesia Thailand	Fouracre & Maunder 1977; Fouracre 1977; Bhandhachat 1979.
Becak, Samlor Trishaw, Tricycle Pedicab	Bicycle Rickshaw Manual Power 2-3 Passengers	0.4	Thailand Indonesia Malaysia Philippines	Meier 1977; Forbes 1978; Rimmer 1978 & 1982; Soegijoko 1979; Kartodirajo 1981.
Public Autos	Taxis & all other Motorised Paratransit (Bemo, Jeepney, Minibus, Autorickshaw)	—	All ASEAN Countries	Fouracre 1977; Ocampo 1982 a&b; Bovy & Kreyenbuhl 1976; Pendakur 1976 & 1981 a&b; Roth & Wynn 1982; Grava 1978.
Subway/Metro	Rapid Transit Train (800-2500 Passengers Per Train)	Peak Hr: 2.2 Off-Peak: 4.7	Manila (under construction) Singapore (planning stage)	Republic of the Philippines 1982; Pendakur 1982.
City Bus Stage-Bus	Standard Passenger Bus (55-90 Passengers Per Bus)	Peak Hr: 3.8 Off-Peak: 7.0	All ASEAN Countries	Fiebel & Walters 1980; Pendakur 1982; Krynetr 1981; Marler 1982.

* Adapted from Bendixson (1974), Owen (1973), and author's data files.

enterprises owned less than five units (Allport 1976). Since 1976, the government has been aggressively encouraging the individual entrepreneurs to join transport co-operatives. It is estimated that in 1981, about 25% of the jeepney units in Manila belonged to co-operatives.

In the case of small vehicles such as the jeepney, tricycle, **bemo, becak, helicak**, minibus, **samlor, silor** (Table 3), it is possible to keep the fleet size small and the operation fiercely competitive. However, it is extremely difficult for a single bus to serve one route completely in any major city. This is the reason that route associations are popular and successful. The route is shared by the members of the association. Each member owns his own vehicle, maintains it, operates it and receives the revenues from that operation (for example, the minibuses in Kuala Lumpur).

The size of the fleet and the organizational structure are critically important in maintaining efficient and economic urban transport services. Smaller fleet sizes and the informal organization (family units) enable the system not only to respond quickly to variations in demand but also to provide a service at low cost. The co-operatives and route associations can assist in training and banking but when co-operatives become large corporate entities, the danger exists that competition will fade and costs will soar.

System Structure and Vehicle Size

It used to be taken for granted that larger vehicles, that is buses (economies of scale), were more efficient due to savings in costs on a passenger/km basis. However, recent research indicates that minibuses (smaller vehicles) have proven to be as efficient and more profitable in Kuala Lumpur (Walters 1979). This is because higher loads and higher speeds have been achieved by the minibuses in Kuala Lumpur. They were introduced in 1974-75 to meet the transport needs that regular buses could not satisfy (Table 3). The minibuses are very popular with the travelling public and hence quite profitable even though they are operating on less favoured routes. The authorities have now limited the number to 400 in order to protect the revenues of the regular franchised bus system. Evidence from Manila also suggests that costs per passenger/km are about the same for a jeepney as for a bus (Roth 1980). In essence, the smaller vehicles, comprising the secondary urban transport system (Table 3), can operate efficiently and compete effectively with the larger vehicle (bus) systems.

Energy efficiency (Table 3) is an important consideration in the selection of vehicles. Research on energy consumption and characteristics of secondary transport vehicles is very sparse. However, there is emerging evidence to indicate that, contrary to common perception, public buses and subways are not necessarily more energy efficient than small secondary transport vehicles. Data presented in Table 3 show that smaller vehicles are substantially more energy efficient although they cannot handle the very large loads in limited road/track space. However, the small vehicles can compete effectively under selective load circumstances.

Smaller vehicles have several other advantages: they are easier to fill, load and unload; they stop less frequently and for a shorter time; they can be manoeuvred easily and are, therefore, more efficient on congested streets; and a disabled vehicle means the loss of only a small amount of seat/km. Furthermore, smaller vehicles are easier to build because they are generally bought off the shelf and altered as required (such as the minibus and **silor**) or built locally from various components (such as the jeepney). Therefore, the smaller vehicles have an important and efficient role within the urban transport system.

System Characteristics

Although there has been continued high growth in the number of private vehicles (cars, motor-cycles and bicycles) during the last two decades in ASEAN, the public transport component is still the backbone of the urban transport system. It now consists of standard buses complemented by a variety of secondary transport vehicles of different sizes, capacities, and energy constraints (Table 3).

The jeepney, a converted jeep with a seating capacity of 6-20 persons, is a common vehicle in the Philippines. In recent years, the tricycle has become quite popular for link trips (from home to the nearest public transport route or terminal). The tricycle is a three-wheeled, two or three-seater vehicle, manually driven like a bicycle. It is also called a **trishaw** or pedicab in Malaysia, **becak** in Indonesia, **samlor** in Thailand.

Minibuses are small buses, which could be converted vans. They are common in Malaysia, Thailand, and Indonesia. It is called a microbus in Indonesia and a queue bus in Thailand, and can seat 6-16 passengers. The opelet is a smaller version of the minibus. It is a converted van with 6-8 seats and is common in Indonesia.

23

A **helicak** is a two-seater, three-wheeled pedicab, driven by a motor-cycle engine. It is also called a **bajaj** and is common in Indonesia. A **bemo** is a larger **helicak**, also prevalent in Indonesia. A **silor** in Thailand is the same as a **bemo**.

All the secondary transport vehicles shown in Table 3 are indigeneous local versions of a bicycle, motor-cycle, van or jeep. They have been developed over the past four decades to suit local enterprise, tastes and vehicle availability. The energy efficiency, on the basis of energy consumed per passenger/km, is approximately the same for all secondary transport vehicles except the **becak**. The **becak** is twice as energy efficient as other secondary transport modes. This is because of the human motive power.

Table 4 shows the characteristics of the public transport system in selected cities of ASEAN. Buses in all the cities operate in the traditional fashion with fixed fares, stops, and routes. The carrying capacity varies depending on vehicle type, but ranges from 45-85 persons.

Buses are not permitted to operate in Bandung. They provide only the inter-city service. Public transport is essentially supplied by the microbus and the **becak**. But the microbus system operates like a standard bus system: with fixed fares, stops and routes.

Jakarta's public transport system consists of buses and a vast range of secondary transport vehicles. The minibuses, with a carrying capacity of 20 passengers, operate on a fixed fares, stops, and route system. The opelet operates on fixed routes on a demand responsive basis with fixed fares, whereas the **bemo** operates in a similar fashion but with negotiated fares. The **bajaj** and **becak** operate on a demand responsive basis on any route with negotiated fares like a taxi. Surabaya's public transport system consists of buses, **bemos**, and **becaks** operating in a similar way to those in Jakarta.

Kuala Lumpur's public transport system consists of buses and minibuses. Buses operate on fixed routes, with fixed fares and stops. Minibuses operate on fixed routes and fares but on a demand responsive basis. The buses have up to 56 seats whereas minibuses have only 16.

The jeepneys of Manila operate like the minibuses of Kuala Lumpur. The tricycles operate on demand on any route with a negotiated fare. The transport system in Chiang Mai depends upon minibuses with 12-14 seats operating on variable routes on fixed fares but on a demand basis. The **samlors** provide service like a taxi, on negotiated fares.

TABLE 4

Public Transport System Characteristics

City	Population (in millions)	Vehicle type & Number	Passenger Capacity	Method of Operation Routes	Stops	Fare	Sources
Bandung (1976)	1.3	Microbus 2,800	16-15	Fixed	Fixed	Fixed	Soegijoko 1979.
		Becak 12,400	2	Variable	Demand	Negotiated	
Jakarta (1977)		Bus 2,400	45-60	Fixed	Fixed	Fixed	Dick 1981 a&b.
		Minibus 1,000	20	Fixed	Fixed	Fixed	Case & Latchford 1981.
		Opelet 3,000	9	Fixed	Demand	Negotiated	
		Bemo 9,800	7	Fixed	Demand	Negotiated	
		BajaJ 1,900	2	Variable	Demand	Negotiated	
		Becak 1,400	2	Variable	Demand	Negotiated	
Surabaya (1976)	2.3	Bus 70	45-55	Fixed	Fixed	Fixed	Halcrow Fox 1977.
		Bemo 2,000	7-11	Fixed	Demand	Fixed	
		Becak 37,000	2	Variable	Demand	Negotiated	
Kuala Lumpur (1978)	1.0	Bus 440	56	Fixed	Fixed	Fixed	Case & Latchford 1981.
		Minibus 400	16	Fixed	Demand	Fixed	
Manila (1980)	5.9	Bus 5,800	16-75	Fixed	Fixed	Fixed	Republic of the
		Jeepney 37,000	18-16	Fixed	Fixed	Fixed	Philippines 1982.
		Tricycles 13,000	2	Demand	Demand	Negotiated	
Bangkok (1981)	5.3	Bus & Minibus 18,360	Bus:45-85 Minibus:14-50	Fixed	Fixed	Fixed	JICA 1982.
		Taxi & Samlor 21,400	Taxi:4	Demand	Demand	Negotiated	
		Silor *	Samlor:2 7	Demand	Demand	Negotiated	
				Demand	Demand	Negotiated	
Chiang Mai (1977)	0.15	Bus 42	24-30	Fixed	Fixed	Fixed	Case & Latchford 1981.
		Minibus 2,200	10-12	Variable	Demand	Fixed	
		Samlor 1,000	2	Variable	Demand	Negotiated	

* Data not available.

Taxis are available in all the ASEAN cities. Fares are negotiated in Bangkok, Jakarta, and Kuala Lumpur, but in Manila and Singapore they are metered.

IV

URBAN TRAVEL IN ASEAN

Bandung

There has been a steady growth of public and private transport supply in Bandung during the past decade. A large number of people walk, especially when they are not required to carry heavy hand baggage. Soegijiko's survey indicates that in 1978, 59% of all trips in Bandung were made on foot (Soegijoko 1979).

Motorization has been increasing rapidly in recent years. During the period 1972-77, private cars increased by 207%. The ownership rate was higher than in Jakarta and comparable to any other ASEAN city (Table 5). During the same period, motor-cycles increased by 233%, providing Bandung's higher income residents with better motorized mobility. At the same time, the lower income groups were also increasing their stock of non-motorized personal vehicles -- bicycles. Bicycles increased by 36% in five years. Private transport was used for 48% of all trips (excluding walking). Private cars accounted for 14%, motor-cycles 23%, and bicycles 11% (Table 5). The high ratio of private-transport trips indicates the affluence of the population, the rate of vehicle ownership, and lack of adequate public transport supply.

The public transport system in Bandung has evolved over the last thirty years in a similar manner to that in Surabaya and Jakarta. There has been a consistent effort to abolish secondary transport vehicles, particularly the non-motorized types (the **becak**), but unfortunately without providing an adequate alternative supply of public transport. Because buses are not allowed to operate in the city, public transport consists mainly of micro/minibuses and **becaks.**

There were 35 minibuses and 2,800 microbuses operating in Bandung in 1976. Registered **becaks** numbered 12,400 in Bandung in

27

TABLE 5

Urban Travel: Public and Private Modes

City	Population ('000)	Cars & Motor-cycles per 1000 persons	Modal Split for Motorized trips		Share of Public Transport		Sources
			by Private Vehicles ($)	by Public Vehicles ($)	By Bus ($)	By Secondary Transport ($)	
Bandung, INDONESIA	1,300[a] (1976)	100[b] (cars 35) (1976)	48[b] cars 14 motor-cycles 23 bicycles 11	52[b]	_[b]	52[b] microbus 25 becak 25 minibus 1 taxi 1	a. Salih 1981. b. Soegijoko 1979.
Jakarta, INDONESIA	6,000[a] (1977)	72[a] (cars 25) (1977)	35[b]	65[b]	32[b]	minibus 10[a,b] opelet 10 taxis,etc. 13	a. Case & Latchford 1981. b. Rimmer & Dick 1980.
Surabaya, INDONESIA	2,300[a] (1976)	62[a] (cars 11) (1976)	64[a] cars 16 motor-cycle 48	36[a]	5[a]	minibus & bemo 15[a] becak 16	a. Halcrow Fox 1977.
Kuala Lumpur, MALAYSIA	1,000[a] (1978)	150[b] (cars 90) (1978)	53[a] cars 39 motor-cycle 14	47[a]	19[a]	minibus 19[a] taxi 9	a. Case & Latchford 1981. b. Jamieson McKay 1981.
Manila, PHILIPPINES	5,900[a] (1980)	52[a] (cars 45) (1980)	25[a] cars 25 motor-cycle negligible	75[a]	15[a]	jeepney 50[a] tricycle 9 taxi 1	a. Republic of Philippines 1982.
Bangkok, THAILAND	5,330[a] (1981)	116[a] (cars 62) (1981)	28[a] cars 22 motor-cycles 6	72[a]	60[a]	samlor 2[a] taxi 1 minibus 9	a. JICA 1982.
Chiang Mai, THAILAND	150[a] (1977)	40[b,c] (cars 5) (1977)	7[a]	93[a]	7[a]	minibus 80 samlor 6	a. Fouracre & Maunder 1977. b. ESCAP 1982. c. Suntaranont 1982.

1976, but the police estimated that there were 30,000 **becaks** operating in the city (Soegijoko 1979). There were also 60 taxis. Public transport was used for 52% of all vehicular trips: microbus 25%, minibus 1%, taxi 1% and **becaks** 25%. Motor-cycles, microbuses and **becaks** account for about three-quarters of total person trips by vehicles in Bandung.

Jakarta

Jakarta, the largest city in ASEAN, made the same mistake as many other Western cities and abolished the tramways in the late fifties. However, the gap left by the removal of trams was not filled by providing additional public transport capacity. The vacuum created by increasing demand and decreasing supply was informally filled by pirate unlicensed **opelets** and **bemos** operating more or less along the old tram routes. By 1974, the government-owned bus company PPD was operating 600 buses. Together with privately owned bus companies, there were 2,400 buses operating by 1979 (Table 4). The public bus service in Jakarta is now being provided by one government-owned company (PPD) and 14 other private operators. Although the PPD fleet consists of 600 buses, they generally have only one-third to half of their fleet in service.

In 1976, the government decided to establish another public corporation, PT Metro Mini, for the sole purpose of operating a minibus fleet. This fleet was supposed to replace both legal and illegal **opelets** and **bemos** operating on routes where standard buses could not (lower density areas, narrow streets, etc). The aim was to modernize and introduce greater efficiency. There were 1,000 minibuses and 3,000 **opelets** in service in 1979 (Table 4). Later, the government decided to replace the informal indigeneous **opelets** by modern mikrolets (converted Mitsubishi Colts) and by 1981, 800 of these new vehicles were in operation.

There were still 9,800 **bemos** and 1,900 **bajaj** operating in 1979, and 1,400 **becaks** were also in service. However, it should be noted that in Jakarta, unlike other Indonesian cities, the **becak** is confined strictly to night-time operation and otherwise to the edges of the city. It has been an explicit policy to replace the **becaks** with motorized vehicles.

There are now about 6,000 taxis in operation in Jakarta and they are available reasonably readily. Fares are still negotiated and most taxis do not use meters.

Nearly two-thirds (65%) of all motorized person trips are by

29

public transport vehicles which comprise only 4% of the total vehicles in Jakarta (**Wheel Extended**, 1979e). Buses and minibuses with only 3,400 vehicles account for 42% of the trips (Tables 4 and 5). Nearly 50% of all public transport trips in Jakarta are by secondary transport vehicles (Table 5). Although the government is in a very strong position to mandate any vehicle/system out of existence, the secondary transport services persist because of both a lack of adequate transport supply and the flexible service provided by them.

Surabaya

Surabaya's urban transport system has grown in a similar fashion to that of Jakarta. For most major decisions in Surabaya, Jakarta is used as the model. Tramways were replaced by a fleet of buses in 1965. By 1970, there had been considerable growth in the number of **bemos**, although the **becak** was still continuing to provide good service. Until about 1975, public transport was essentially by **bemo** and **becak.**

It has been the explicit policy in Surabaya, as in Jakarta, to phase out the **becak** with motorized vehicles. While **bemos** would replace the **becak**, it was planned to replace the **bemos** on the main routes by buses and minibuses. This was the essence of the policy of motorization and fleet modernization. By 1979, the **becak** operations had been controlled, with one-third of the vehicles restricted to night-time use only, and the remaining for day and night use. No new licences have been issued since 1973.

Public transport supply in Surabaya is inadequate. For a population of 2.3 million, there were only 70 buses and 2,000 **bemos** in 1976 (Table 4), while 37,000 **becaks** provided the slow but required service. By 1980, 190 buses were operating (Dick 1981b). As the buses displaced the **bemo** on major routes, the **bemo** displaced the **becak**. Additional service with better speeds has benefited the users, and new **bemo** routes have emerged in response to market demand (Dick 1981b).

Residents of Surabaya have to depend on private transport because of a lack of public transport supply and the low quality when available. Two-thirds of all person trips are made on private vehicles. Nearly half (48%) of the trips are by motor-cycle which has emerged as a common vehicle in Surabaya (Table 5). Although motor-cycle ownership rates are not much higher than in KL and Bangkok, the trip rates are significantly higher.

It was estimated that there were 200,000 bicycles in Surabaya in 1976 (Halcrow Fox 1977). Because of a lack of sufficient public transport supply, the bicycles were used extensively by the middle and lower income groups, particularly students. Unfortunately, the major transportation studies done during the past decade at considerable expense do not provide any information on travelling on foot or on bicycles. The roads and foot-paths for the pedestrians and cyclists are in very poor condition.

For short length link trips (from 1.0 to 1.5 km), the most popular vehicle is the **becak**. The **bemo** and motor-cycle are used for trips between 2.0 and 2.5 km. Buses and minibuses are used for longer trips because of the poor frequency and service. The average distance of a bus trip is 4.5 km.

Kuala Lumpur (KL)

The growth in motorization (ownership of motorized private vehicles - cars and motor-cycles) has far exceeded the population growth rate in Kuala Lumpur during the past decade. The annual growth rate for motorization has been about 11% while the population has increased about 5%. In 1978, there were 90 cars per 1,000 persons and 60 motor-cycles per 1,000 persons (Jamieson McKay 1981).

Although the public transport system in KL was adequate during the 1950s and 1960s, it had deteriorated by 1974. Buses were overloaded and had irregular schedules due to traffic congestion and/or frequent breakdowns. There were eight private companies operating the system without government subsidies but under regulated franchises. In 1974, the fares were increased slightly and the companies were granted a reduction in taxes to enable them to expand their fleets (**Wheel Extended,** 1979b).

In 1976, the World Bank suggested that an introduction of minibuses under private ownership could relieve congestion. The Bank also recommended additional private car restraint measures (taxes, parking levy) and an area licensing scheme similar to that in Singapore to reduce the number of cars entering the central area. Since then, the government has implemented the minibus scheme, and a modified version of taxes and parking fees to curb automobile use. However, the central area licensing scheme has been shelved for future consideration (**Wheel Extended,** 1979b).

In spite of improved public transport, KL has a very high

rate of private vehicle use, accounting for 53% of all person trips (mainly cars and motor-cycles). Cars accounted for 39% of total person trips and motor-cycles, 14%. Such high use of private cars has resulted in heavy congestion in the central area of KL.

The public transport system consists primarily of buses, minibuses and taxis. Buses carry 19% of total person trips and minibuses another 19%. Minibuses, which have a seating capacity of 16 seats each and no standing permitted, are very popular. The buses operate in the traditional manner and are often overloaded. The fares and routes of both are controlled by the government. There were 400 buses and 400 minibuses in operation in 1978.

Minibuses are popular with the users because they are perceived as comfortable, convenient, fast, and reasonably priced. Unless there is a vacant seat, a passenger cannot get on it. The minibuses are owned by operators with small fleets. They are also more profitable than the buses and are demand responsive. The authorities currently limit their number to protect the regular franchised standard buses. As a consequence, the fortunate owners of minibus licences obtain substantial financial returns from their vehicles (Roth 1982).

The 400 minibuses operate on 17 designated routes. Two-thirds (65%) of the licences are held by single-unit enterprises and the largest number of units in one enterprise is 30. The minibus operation and its profitability in KL clearly shows that the traditional assumptions -- that public transport should be both a public enterprise and a large enterprise -- are myths. It also shows that smaller units, under proper circumstances, can compete quite well with bigger units and bigger enterprises. A recent World Bank study indicates that minibus operations can be cost effective, produce a high annual rate of return on capital (133%) and can be significant components of plans to reduce central area congestion (Walters 1979).

Manila

The traffic situation in Manila has progressively deteriorated since 1970 with increases in the number of motor vehicles and their use and little or no improvements to the road network. While the bus fleet has deteriorated, there has been a substantial increase in the number of jeepneys, both legal and illegal.

The motor vehicle fleet has doubled since 1975, with private cars increasing by 60% and jeepneys by 250%. The bus fleet, however, has decreased from 4,000 units to 2,000 units. At the same time, public transport use has increased by 69% from 6.2 million trips in 1975 to 10.5 million trips in 1980 (Dent 1981). Public transport system components are largely private enterprise units. There is only one publicly owned and subsidized bus company, the MMTC.

The most popular form of public transport is the jeepney. It operates on fixed routes and with variable fares (according to distance travelled) regulated by the government in a similar way to the buses. It picks up passengers, on demand, literally anywhere. Headways are short (often only one minute) and thus the users are assured of a high frequency service. The passengers may need to make transfers but the walking distance between the routes is usually very short (200m). The load factor of the jeepneys often exceed 80%, and the average trip distance is 4-5km.

Most of the demand responsive systems in Western countries, such as the minibus/telebus/dial-a-bus services which are generally publicly owned, have become very high cost services and some have failed. However, the jeepneys of Manila under private ownership continue to provide high quality service under highly competitive circumstances, and continue to make a profit.

Recent studies show that when all the work and school trips are considered (including walking), 8% walk, 10% go by car, 17% by bus, 60% by jeepney, and 6% by other means (motor-cycle, taxi, bicycle) (Dent 1981). When only the trips by vehicles are taken into account (that is, excluding walking) 25% go by private vehicles (cars and motor-cycles), 50% by jeepney, 15% by bus, 9% by tricycle and 1% by taxi. Bicycles are not common in Manila (Table 5).

Although Manila has had a high rate of growth in private vehicle ownership, the rate of increase of private cars has been tapering off in recent years (Republic of the Philippines 1982). It has been suggested that the rate of growth of future car ownership will not be as high as in the past because apart from high fuel cost and purchase prices, the very small segment of the population that can afford cars already have one (World Bank 1981). Under these circumstances, the vast majority of Manila's population will continue to depend upon public transport, particularly the secondary transport -- jeepney.

An LRT system is under construction in Manila, and is expected to open for service by September 1984. It is estimated to cost about US$300 million when fully completed. The line and

33

stations are elevated for its entire length of 15 km. The fare is expected to be kept low, at one peso (US$0.09), thus requiring capital and/or operating subsidies.

Bangkok

Traffic congestion in Bangkok has often been described as being among the worst in the world. Traffic is heavy throughout much of the day and there are no well-defined traffic peaks as in other ASEAN cities. Travel speeds are very low, often averaging less than 15 km/h and can sometimes be well below 10 km/h. Travel times can vary greatly on the same routes. Bangkok's arterial streets operate at low levels of service for much of the working day. During five and a half hours of the day, traffic conditions are unstable, often in a state of forced flow (Jones et al. 1982).

Bangkok is the only major ASEAN city with manually operated traffic controls at various central area intersections without interconnections. The traffic police operate the controls on long cycles, causing traffic to back up for several blocks along all streets. The situation is almost equal to designed congestion.

Motorization has been occurring in Bangkok at a high rate in the past few years. A recent study conservatively predicted that motorization will increase from a level of 44 cars per 1,000 persons in 1978 to 55 cars in 1990. This forecast presumed that the government would implement major policies to reduce traffic congestion by introducing severe restrictions on private car use and/or parking in the central area. Based on these assumptions, it was predicted that traffic volumes would increase by 56% by 1990 and by 100% by 2000 (ERTAT 1979).

In 1983, Bangkok did not have any major restraints on either the ownership or the use of the private car. As a result, motorization and car use have outpaced all previous forecasts. In 1981, there were already 62 cars per 1,000 persons (Table 5). It is now forecast that the traffic volume in 1990 will be double that of 1980 (JICA 1982). Based upon these new forecasts, the government has decided to build a new MRT system prior to introducing any traffic restraints or controls. This MRT system, if completed in 1996, will be 50 km long, and is expected to cost US$600-800 million.

Public transport efficiency suffers greatly in Bangkok because there are no priority measures for transit, and traffic controls are archaic. Automobile use is unrestrained and the very limited street space is shared by a confusing mix of slow, fast, big, and small vehicles. The average day-time traffic speeds in 1981 varied from 16 to 28 km/h along ten major corridors even at a distance of 10 km from the centre of the city. Not only has traffic congestion spread spatially from the centre but also temporally from the peak periods to the middle of the day and often into the evening as well (Cundill and Byrne 1982).

Despite growing motorization, private car ownership is beyond the means of 95% of the population. They have no choice but to depend upon public transport. In 1981, 72% of all person trips (excluding walking) were by public transport (Table 5). Buses were the backbone of the public transport system, carrying 60% of all person trips (83% of all public transport trips). There were 18,360 buses in 1981 (standard and mini) operated by the Bangkok Mass Transit Authority (BMTA). During the period 1970-75, 16 different private bus companies with diverse routes and vehicles were consolidated under a single public corporation, the BMTA. The BMTA buses are aging, overloaded and badly maintained. The fares are kept artificially low at 1.5 baht for the first 10 km (US$0.065) and 0.5 baht for the next 10 km in ordinary buses. The minibuses and airconditioned buses charge substantially more.

Samlors (motorized and pedalled) are registered as taxis and therefore adequate data on their number, growth, and ownership patterns are not available. In 1972, there were 7,000 **samlors**. It is estimated that there were 10,000 **samlors** in 1981. The motorized **samlors** provide a competing service with the taxis and are generally owned by individuals rather than corporations. They are demand responsive, and carried only 2% of the total person trips in 1981 (Table 5). Minibuses accounted for 9% of the total, and taxis only 1%. In contrast, the BMTA buses carried 60% of all trips.

Chiang Mai

Chiang Mai is small compared to other ASEAN cities and is the second largest city in Thailand. The motorization rate is very low at 5 cars per 1,000 persons and almost everybody has to depend upon public transport. The motor-cycle ownership has been increasing rapidly and was 35 per 1,000 persons in 1977. Only 7% of the total person trips (excluding walking) are made by private vehicles (Table 5).

The public transport system in Chiang Mai consists primarily of minibuses, also called **silors**. Similar to the Manila jeepneys in design, the Chiang Mai **silors** are converted Mazda or Daihatsu vehicles, which can seat 10-12 passengers. Profits appear to be good and minibus drivers jealously guard their independence. Most drivers (93%) are also owners of their vehicles. There are hardly any bureaucratic regulations governing minibus operations and government controls are minimal. In fact, the operators themselves have informally organized the system, operate in competition, and appear to respond quickly to demand changes (Fouracre and Maunder 1977).

Public transport accounts for 93% of all trips, of which only 7% are by bus. This is primarily because there were only 42 buses operating in 1977 (Table 4). **Samlors** provide a useful service in areas where minibuses are not operating.

In Chiang Mai, there are two kinds of **silors**: the minibus and the queue minibus. A total of 1,370 minibuses operate from different activity centres (terminals) with no fixed routes, and the passengers use it primarily as a shared taxi, the route being determined by the majority of the passengers. A flat fare is charged for all trips in the city (2 bahts in 1977). The competition is fierce, the organization is informal, and more than half of the minibuses in service operate without a licence. The minibus accounts for 78% of all person trips (84% of all public transport trips).

The queue minibus system is more formally organized. There are 830 queue minibuses operating on several fixed routes. The fare structure is also fixed at 2 bahts (US$0.087) for the first 10 km and 1 baht for the next 10 km. Although there were 830 vehicles operating, they carried only 2% of the total person trips.

There were 1,800 **samlors** providing service in areas not reached by the minibuses and occasionally competing along the same routes. They carried only 6% of total trips (Table 4 and 5). The number of **samlors** in Chiang Mai has been decreasing steadily from 2,700 in 1970 to approximately 1,000 in 1977 (Fouracre and Maunder 1977). They operate on any route, with negotiated fares.

V

URBAN TRANSPORT POLICY

Urban Transport Goals

The basic function of urban transport is to provide efficient (economic and social) links between home and work, and producers and users of goods and services. The level of accessibility and mobility provided must be commensurate with the level of service in other urban functions. The efficiency and the cost of urban transport affects directly almost all other urban functions, be it fire protection, policing, drainage, water supply, public health, or education. Urban transport policy, therefore, has considerable effect on the cost of other urban services. At the same time, urban transport requirements are essentially predetermined by broad land use policies: strong centre/weak centre, urban/suburban, segregated/combined land uses, self-sufficient competing tour centres, single/multiple centre, day-time/night-time populations, etc. It is necessary, therefore, to clearly understand the relationship between land use policies and the resultant urban form which predetermines, to a large extent, the urban transport costs.

It is necessary and important to deliberately pursue and encourage the land use patterns that reduce the number and the distance of motorized trips. Even though the task is complex and difficult, it is necessary to try to achieve minimization of motorized transport needs by encouraging a balanced distribution of employment opportunities throughout the urban area. This is certainly not a panacea for all urban transport problems but will assist in reducing overall transport costs. As the cities grow in size and complexity, it is important to revise the land use policies to suit the future scenarios rather than pursue policies that reflect the past.

Achieving the critical optimization between land use and transport is easier said than done. While most urban development takes place within the private sector, the extent to which the private sector understands and interprets government policies has a significant influence on the spatial aspects of urban development and, therefore, urban transport. Thus, it is important for the public sector to clearly enunciate the urban transport goals and make sure that urban transport policies are derived from those goals.

Cities with populations of one to two million, such as KL, tend to be mononuclear, with most employment opportunities concentrated in one centre or along one axis. Larger cities, such as Manila and Bangkok, are often characterized by multinuclear employment concentrations. The government policies and how clearly they are perceived by the private sector as to future economic and spatial patterns have a significant influence on private sector investment strategies. For example, in multinuclear Manila (Makati, Quezon, and Ermita), the centre (Ermita) is very congested with very high levels of activity. Although it has been government policy for a decade to move various government functions to Quezon, it is yet to happen and many movable government departments are still in the centre. As a result, the private sector has not made any major investments in Quezon. The costs of congestion in the centre continue to increase while at the same time large investments are being made in new transport systems (LRT). The mere existence of a land use plan is not enough. It is essential to follow up with clearly articulated policies and government actions to demonstrate the political will to implement the plan so that private sector investments can follow. Although the balance between land use costs and transport costs is a delicate one, the goals to minimize the latter should be clearly stated and followed, albeit each city will require unique policies to suit its own socio-economic environment.

Taming the Automobile

The discussion presented earlier shows that recent population growths in major ASEAN cities have been accompanied by very high rates of growth in the number of private cars and motor-cycles. There is evidence also to support the view that the ASEAN countries have not tried seriously or are unwilling to try to curb the high growth of private cars. Whether it is the lack of political will or effective lobbying by auto-oriented groups, many proposals to reduce the growth of private automobiles have not been implemented (for example, KL and Bangkok). The exception is Singapore which implemented a variety of policies to discourage the ownership and use of private automobiles in 1975, including a strict Area Licensing Scheme (ALS) for cars entering the central business district during the morning peak hours.

Increase in the ownership and use of private vehicles is a natural result of higher incomes, and the universal desire for increased mobility. These priorities are expressed as a function of free access, social status and easy mobility in addition to comfort, convenience, safety, and time saving. The question is not to prevent people from buying their own vehicles but to make certain that private vehicle ownership and use are not subsidized by non-users and that private vehicles are charged their fair share of the economic (facilities) and social (environment) costs of catering to their easy use. Traditionally, urban transport investment and taxation policies have heavily subsidized cars and car users. If additional large public investments are required because of private vehicles, then those costs should be recovered from the users (or at least a fair portion of the costs). Emphasis in the past has been on general arterial/highway construction mainly to provide additional road capacity for the smooth and efficient flow of automobiles. Future policy should emphasize the movement of people and goods and not necessarily vehicles alone. Congestion cost for all vehicles and equitable charges for the use of road space must be incorporated into transport pricing structures.

It is important to consider further the limitation of private vehicle use. In the already congested city centres of ASEAN, any additional road capacity can only be created at very high incremental cost. Even if these costs are absorbed by general taxation, the social costs (pollution, safety) of additional vehicles in already congested areas could be very high.

Given the physiographic limitation of the central business districts of the ASEAN cities (rivers, railways, sea, soft soils), additional road capacity will require massive land acquisition, bridges, and road construction. Even if this was possible, given the automobile technology of today, there are critical limits to the further expansion of traffic and/or land use activities.

The experience in ASEAN suggests that the successful policies pursued by Singapore since 1975 in controlling the growth and limiting the use of private vehicles during high congestion periods are of relevance for application in Manila, Bangkok, Jakarta, and KL. It is estimated that if the Singapore ALS had not been implemented in 1975, it would have required in 1983 additional road improvements amounting to US$150-200 million just to keep up with the growing traffic. It is important to note that city centre transport policies must include, as a comprehensive measure, road-user taxes (to discourage use),

39

parking restrictions (to discourage accumulation), alternative modes of public transport, and ownership taxes (to discourage). All these components must be implemented together with compatible land use and zoning policies.

Intellectual and Material Technology

To a large degree, the intellectual technology (methods of analysis) in urban transport planning in ASEAN has been copied from the experience of the developed industrial nations. Benefits derived from investments in transport are generally in time, cost, comfort and convenience, and safety. The largest benefit is in time saving. However, several basic questions remain unanswered. Do time savings have equal monetary value for all persons and what increments of time savings are of significance to whom? Should we assume that everyone is expected to devote a certain amount of time (say 20 minutes) to travel from home to work (irrespective of the mode) and, therefore, time savings up to that point (20 minutes) have no monetary value as benefits? At what point (travel time) does fatigue affect productivity? Although it is basic knowledge that the value of time and money is significantly different for different income groups, the current analytical methods assume straight line values regardless of income or travel time.

For the urban poor, the availability and cost of transport are very important. By definition, the poor are essentially at the margin of subsistence and are particularly vulnerable to disruptions in their incomes induced by inefficient or costly transport. Furthermore, the urban transport sector in the ASEAN countries provides employment for a large portion of the population (Pendakur 1976, World Bank 1975). It is important, therefore, to consider who pays for improved transport systems and how?

All of the major urban transport studies in ASEAN during the past decade have been done by foreign consultants, often with token local partnership. It is interesting to note that a Japanese consultant will compare the ASEAN conditions to Japan (Manila and Tokyo), a German consultant to Germany (Surabaya and Frankfurt), and a British consultant to the United Kingdom (KL and London). It is a fallacy to use such comparisons because the value systems are vastly different, although we can learn from comparisons. It is very important that studies compare various ASEAN experiences and extend theory and practice from such comparisons rather than simply rely on comparisons to high-income cities in other regions.

40

In some instances, socio-economic analysis is highly distorted by the foreign consultants especially if they have links with foreign aid/trade agencies. Because the primary goal of the agency is foreign aid/trade, unrealistic and totally non-market interest rates and repayment periods are used to provide an acceptable benefit/cost ratio. Very low interest rates distort the benefit/cost analysis and render marginal projects justifiable. For example, one study used an interest rate of 2% per annum, and even this interest was forgiven for the first seven years, and the repayment period stretched over the next forty years (Japan OCTA 1973). Under \such charitable financing conditions, almost any project can be justified. Such methods of analysis distort urban development priorities and seriously affect the land use system. It is necessary, therefore, that the socio-economic components of the analysis reflect the normal ASEAN condition.

Most of the material technology, the vehicles and parts, are imported. Private cars, in particular, are almost always imported. In the case of secondary transport (Table 3), however, there are large domestic multipliers to the economy. For example, large numbers of people are employed in the jeepney industry in Manila, and the industry is only moderately dependent on external factors (Pendakur 1976). Since economic conditions and unemployment rate vary widely within the region (for example, Singapore vs Thailand), the questions of employment, foreign exchange, savings and energy conservation must be resolved in a larger national context. The analytical methods used in the studies are derived from Western countries where similar problems do not exist.

Transition to High Technology and Secondary Transport

Recent demographic studies indicate that the populations of all the ASEAN cities except Singapore will continue to grow at an annual rate of 2-3% (Chapter II, Salih 1981; U.N. Secretariat 1980). Irrespective of whether or not the income and employment levels improve, the demand for travel will increase commensurate with population growth. Should there be net increases in the incomes of the poor, then travel demand will grow even further. In the process of growth and the resultant provision of higher transport capacity, high technology improvements should and will be made. Currently, Manila is expecting to complete its new 23km LRT system by September 1984, Singapore has begun construction of its MRT system and Bangkok is designing its new MRT system. These new high technology MRT/LRT systems in the five ASEAN capital cities are expected to cost about US$5-8 billion to build during the 1980-95 period (see Chapter I and III). While transport modernization is a prerequisite to the efficient functioning of any urban system, there are a number of complex socio-economic questions that should be resolved equitably during the transition period. The experiences in Singapore and Hong Kong are quite relevant but need to be modified to suit the unique conditions in other cities. While it was possible to let market forces weed out costly and inefficient transport modes in Singapore (rickshaws), it may not be possible to adopt the **laissez-faire** policy in economies with a high degree of unemployment and high employment multiples.

The secondary transport system (see Table 3 and Chapter III and IV), consisting of a wide variety of vehicles and ownership patterns, plays a very important role in all the ASEAN cities, without which the entire urban transport system would collapse. The system reflects a tremendous vitality and is demand responsive in nature. It is essentially under private ownership, with a large number of owners having very small fleets. In contrast to the publicly owned bus systems, the secondary system is profit-making and the vehicle fleets are in good condition. It provides employment for a large number of people, and has high socio-economic multipliers. There is not only jeepney service and jeepney industry in Manila but also a jeepney culture. A large number of vehicles are unlicensed (illegal) -- nearly 17,000 jeepneys in Manila and 15,000 minibuses in Bangkok. It is estimated that nearly 3.5 million trips per day in Manila and 1.2 million trips per day in Bangkok are made by illegal public transport. If these vehicles were withdrawn from service, it would cause socio-economic as well as transport chaos. Under the current circumstances, the secondary transport system is profit-making, more efficient, more convenient, more demand responsive and more reliable than the publicly owned bus system. Nearly 50%-80% of all public transport trips are made by secondary transport and it is nearly a door-to-door system.

Within the context of transport modernization and the impending onstream of new high technology, large capacity, publicly owned systems within the next few years, a number of major policy questions need to be resolved:

1. Will there be a continuing demand for the secondary transport systems?

2. Will the system be relegated to serving link trips only (that is, from home to LRT/MRT stations, etc.)? If so, how will it affect the incomes of those employed in the system now?

3. If the supply/demand market system reduces the need for

secondary transport and their incomes, will the new
publicly owned, high capacity systems at least break
even? If not, there are two sets of losses.

4. How do we retrain and re-employ those that are displaced
   by the high technology MRT/LRT systems?

5. How does the secondary transport system fit into the
   urban transport plan so that the private sector can plan
   effectively to provide the service?

6. Will the new systems cost more to the consumer directly
   and indirectly?

7. Who pays for improvements and who benefits?

A composite policy framework must be consistent with state
goals of employment, efficiency, and equity. In a poor country
with high unemployment, the employment characteristics of the
secondary system become significant (such as in Thailand and the
Philippines) whereas in a full employment economy, it is not as
important (such as in Singapore).

Several conceptual myths derived from Western countries have
been accepted by ASEAN urban transport planners even though the
historical experience of those countries now suggests otherwise:

1. Public transport is a public good and therefore can only
   be efficiently provided under public ownership. This
   presumes that transport is part of the welfare function
   (like education, and clean water) and public ownership
   by itself can provide efficient and economic service.
   The Western experience of the past decade suggests that
   under public ownership the operating losses have
   increased geometrically and are, in fact, out of
   control. Data presented earlier (see Chapters III and
   IV) show that all the public transport corporations in
   ASEAN are incurring heavy losses whereas parallel
   private systems under unfavourable circumstances can
   make profit (such as the jeepneys of Manila, the
   minibuses of KL). For example, the Bangkok bus system
   (BMTA) incurred an operating loss of US$25 million in
   1979-80 (Fiebel and Walters 1980) and these losses have
   been steadily increasing. There is enough evidence from
   the ASEAN experience to suggest that public ownership
   must be avoided if possible and some governments are
   actively considering such a policy. An example of this
   kind is the recent announcement from Manila that
   indicates the government's desire to dismantle the loss
   incurring Metro Manila Transit Corporation (MMTC).

43

2. The second myth is that the fleet size must be large and under one ownership to provide for economies of scale. This may work under special circumstances in Western countries where procurement and maintenance practices are quite different from those in ASEAN. The ASEAN experience suggests the contrary (see Chapter III). Even though the governments have superimposed several consolidation strategies (such as route associations in KL and co-operatives in Manila), the individual owners with small fleets continue to provide good service and make profit.

3. The third myth is that smaller vehicles are inefficient (in terms of operating cost and energy). This may be quite true if it is assumed that a larger vehicle (bus) is always full. If the average load factors (that is, passenger loads) are considered, the smaller vehicles (jeepney) are, in fact, more efficient. That is the main reason that the jeepneys of Manila can compete with the buses and make a profit.

4. The fourth myth is that the smaller vehicles are not energy efficient. There have been no scholarly examination of vehicle size, occupancy ratio, and energy efficiency. Most research in this area has hitherto been of a censory nature. Data presented in Table 3 show that most secondary transport vehicles are in fact more energy efficient.

Role of Government

The governments have a predominant role and responsibility in planning and providing urban transport. Left to private enterprise alone, the system will not function. However, there are certain urban transport functions that the private sector can perform more efficiently and economically.

There are four general areas of urban transport policy which interrelates to one another in a complex system. Each of these policies affects the other and it has to be formulated in such a way that it is positively complementary. The policy areas are:

a) Planning
b) Investment and Ownership
c) Pricing
d) Regulation
e) System Management

In general, during the period 1960-80, ASEAN urban transport policies have been focused upon:

1. Road and highway construction to accommodate the growing needs of the automobile, particularly in the central business districts.

2. Planning for and acquiring high technology rapid transit systems in a few selected cities (Manila, Bangkok, Singapore).

3. Encouragement of segregated land use and the development of mononuclear (single-centre) growth patterns.

4. Indirectly encouraging automobile ownership and use by having low taxes, access to parking and ample supply of vehicles and parts.

5. Concurrent neglect of public transport services together with restrictions on expansion of additional transport supply by private operators (Manila jeepney).

6. Consolidation and nationalization of private bus operations under public ownership and providing large operating subsidies.

7. Neglect of comprehensive urban transport sector planning and its integration into overall urban development planning and information dissemination to enable the private sector to participate effectively.

The discussion presented in Chapters II to IV represents a broad spectrum of the above policies in the major ASEAN cities. Although many of these policies might have been suitable for the early 1960s, they are certainly not suitable for the foreseeable future, 1980-2000. The urban transport chaos in the central areas cannot be solved by pursuing previous policies but requires policies with a different orientation. These policies should take into consideration the urban transportation goals regarding urban planning, the taming of the automobile, intellectual technology and transition policies for the high technology stage discussed earlier in this chapter. The proposed policy framework can be summarized as follows:

1. Planning

    a) Incorporating urban development goals, with a clear indication of at least the public sector costs of each option and private-sector obligations so that the latter is able to estimate its share of the

45

development costs.

b) Keeping the planning process dynamic and providing continuing mechanisms for consultations between system users and investors.

c) Providing easy access to urban transport data and information without regarding these as "state secrets".

d) Providing a clearly articulated set of urban transport goals and consequences to system users.

e) Seeking non-transport solutions to costly transport investment questions, such as decentralization, mixed land use, self-sufficient town centres, staggered working hours.

f) Requiring that urban transport studies be comprehensive, include all modes (walking, bicycle, motor-cycle, etc.) and that comparative data be from comparable Asian and ASEAN cities.

g) Careful monitoring of various development guide-lines, such as parking provision, so that they do not counteract urban transport goals by encouraging more vehicles to enter already congested areas.

h) Improving environmental management by providing adequate pedestrian pathways, precincts and terminals.

2. Investment and Ownership

a) While the governments will continue to provide and own the way (roads, railway), there must be decreased emphasis on further road construction to cater to more private automobiles, especially in already congested central areas.

b) Careful evaluation of high technology proposals as to their real cost to both the public and private sectors.

c) Emphasis on improving existing public transport facilities, especially buses and minibuses.

d) De-emphasizing in general the consolidation and nationalization (Chapter V) of bus fleets in view of current experience, and encouraging the entry of

46

private operators (such as in KL and Manila) and the elimination of loss producing publicly owned operations.

3. Pricing

a) Exemption of public transport vehicles from heavy taxation to encourage private operators.

b) Removing the determination of bus-fares and taxi-fares from the politically pressured decision-making process and providing a natural system of increases commensurate with cost increases (this will not work in a state monopoly as there will be no efficiency measures to compare).

c) Emphasizing user cost recovery principles by assigning equitable road user taxes to all vehicles commensurate with their road use.

d) Commensurate with the goal to curb the growth of private cars, impose appropriate taxation on ownership and use of all vehicles.

e) Congestion pricing for private vehicles entering already congested central areas during the peak hours, analogous to the successful example of Singapore's Area Licensing Scheme.

4. Regulation

a) Modernizing the regulation of public transport licensing (franchise) system by yearly forecasting of additional franchises available and opening these to competitive tender by private enterprises (such as the minibuses in KL).

b) Comprehensive review of existing regulatory policies and practices affecting the entry of new buses, jeepneys, and other secondary transport with a view to making the entry easier.

c) Strict enforcement of regulations on operations to protect the users (such as on Singapore taxis).

5. System Management

The transport system on the ground has to be managed efficiently with well enforced traffic laws and well designed traffic control systems. If the users and operators perceive that system laws and regulations are not enforced, the obvious result is chaos (such as in Bangkok). If, on the other hand, there is a perception of strict enforcement, the traffic flows smoothly even at the worst of times (such as in Singapore). This will require

a) A comprehensive review of the traffic laws and their modernization.

b) Adequate policing and enforcement by highly trained police personnel.

c) Provision of comprehensive modern interconnected area traffic control.

d) Provision of preferences to public transport vehicles.

e) Improvement of entry/exit conflicts and provision of adequate off-street parking.

f) Provision of fringe parking facilities and pricing them to be attractive to users.

g) Rationalization of routes and the role of secondary transport vehicles with proper separation in systems design for slow moving and fast moving vehicles.

The policies suggested above are not mutually exclusive of each other. They are very much interrelated and each of them affects the others. Therefore, policy formulation and implementation cannot be fragmented and removed from one another. The responsibility and authority for policy formulation and implementation must come together under either one agency or group which should be held liable, in the bureaucratic sense, for system failures. Otherwise, the system can get fragmented and each will work to counteract the other.

Although there is ample evidence that the publicly owned and operated transport systems (bus companies) are not productive (Roth 1977, 1982; Roth and Wynn 1982, Fiebel and Walters 1980), the transition to private operation is not an easy one. This involves public political philosophy and not just economics. However, it must be emphasized that even in countries which are oriented towards public-owned enterprises, ownership plays a minor part in the comprehensive range of policies suggested. The evidence is that, for a variety of reasons, the public systems lose money and are not efficient. Otherwise, they still provide service. The entire spectrum of other policies is more important to urban transport planning.

In ASEAN, comprehensive urban transport planning and administration is very complex and difficult because the authority and responsibility is fragmented among many agencies. The integration of transport planning into overall urban development planning is essential. The systems characteristics of urban transport require that policies be comprehensive and include all modes.

In view of new investments in ASEAN in high technology LRT/MRT systems which are coming on stream in the next few years, the transitional policies are important. How ASEAN cities deal with urban transport predetermines their livability.

VI

FUTURE RESEARCH

This paper has presented, for the first time, urban transport in ASEAN in a comparative way. It has also provided a comprehensive and up-to-date data base for other researchers. Several areas of policy action are suggested for improving urban transport in ASEAN.

The research findings presented here can only be considered indicative and not necessarily definitive. There is an urgent need for further scholarly studies in urban transport. Some of the more important areas of research in ASEAN are:

1. Secondary Transport

    a) energy efficiency;

    b) road space use and cost;

    c) route and price rationalization;

    d) segregation of slow- and fast-moving traffic;

    e) safety.

2. Intellectual Technology

    a) value of time;

    b) analytical methods incorporating secondary transport.

3. Socio-economic Linkages

    a) employment and value multipliers to the economy of various transport modes;

b) socio-economic costs/benefits of private ownership, small fleets, large number of owners;

c) effectiveness of route associations and transport co-operatives.

4. Environmental Design

Incorporating pedestrians and secondary transport.

5. Impact of Modernization

Effect of transport modernization on existing secondary transport users and operators, employment and income distortions, if any, and particularly the impact on the urban poor.

BIBLIOGRAPHY

Books and Monographs

Barwell, I.J., and J.D.G. Howe. **Appropriate Transport Facilities for the Rural Sector in the Developing Countries.** Geneva: International Labour Organization (ILO), 1979.

Beier, George, et al. **The Task Ahead for the Cities of the Developing Countries.** Staff Working Paper No. 209. Washington, D.C.: World Bank, 1975.

Bendixson, T. **Instead of Cars.** London: Temple Smith Ltd., 1974.

Bhandhachat, P. **Low Cost Transportation Study.** Chiangmai, Thailand: Chiangmai University, Social Sciences Research Centre, 1979.

Bovy, Phillipe. **Nonmotorized Urban Transport in Developed and Developing Countries.** Berkeley, Ca.: ITTE, University of California, 1975a.

_____. **Urbanization and Urban Transport Planning in Developing Countries: A Selected Bibliography.** Council of Planning Librarians, Exchange Bibliography No. 835, 1975b.

Bovy, Phillipe, and V. Kreyenbuhl. "Introductory Report" in **Paratransit,** 40th Round Table, European Conference of Ministers of Transport. Paris: Economic Development Centre, OECD, 1976.

Case, D.J., and J.C.R. Latchford. **A Comparison of Public Transport in Cities in South East Asia.** Supplementary Report No. 659. Crowthorne, Berkshire: TRRL, 1981.

52

Chief Statistician. **Yearbook of Statistics, Singapore, 1982/83.**
     Singapore: Department of Statistics, Republic of Singapore,
     1983.

Cundill, M.A., and H.M. Byrne. **A Study of Goods Vehicle
     Restraint in Bangkok.** Supplementary Report No. 733.
     Crowthorne, U.K.: TRRL, 1982.

Eastman, C.R., and D. Pickering. **Transport Problems of the Urban
     Poor in Kuala Lumpur.** Supplementary Report No. 653.
     Crowthorne, U.K.: TRRL, 1981.

Expressway and Rapid Transit Authority of Thailand, Ministry of
     the Interior (ERTAT).   "Mass Rapid Transit System in
     Bangkok". Mimeographed. Bangkok, 1979.

Feibel, Charles and A.A. Walters. **Ownership and Efficiency of
     Urban Buses.** Staff Working Paper No. 371. Washington,
     D.C.: World Bank, 1980.

Forbes, Dean. "Urban-Rural Interdependence: The Trishaws of
     Ujang Pandang". In Peter Rimmer et al., **Food, Shelter and
     Transport in Southeast Asia and the Pacific.** Canberra:
     Australian National University, 1978.

Fouracre, P.R. **Intermediate Public Transport in Developing
     Countries.** Laboratory Report No. 772. Crowthorne, U.K.:
     TRRL, 1977.

Fouracre, P.R., and Maunder, D.A.C. **Public Transport in
     Chiangmai, Thailand.** Supplementary Report No. 285.
     Crowthorne, U.K.: TRRL, 1977.

_____. **Public Transport in Surabaya.** Supplementary Report No.
     370. Crowthorne, U.K.: TRRL, 1978.

_____. **Public Transport Development in Third World Cities.**
     Crowthorne, U.K.: TRRL, 1982.

_____. **A Review of Intermediate Public Transport in Third World
     Cities.** Paper presented at the PTRC Annual Meeting, July
     1979.   Crowthorne, UK: Transport and Road Research
     Laboratory, 1980.

Gakenheimer, R., and P. Bovy. **Urban Transportation Planning in
     Developing Countries - Selected References, Ref. #41.**
     Berkeley, Ca.: ITTE, University of California, 1977.

Grava, Sigurd. **Locally Generated Transportation Modes of the**

Developing World. Special Report No. 181. Washington, D.C.: Transportation Research Board, 1978.

Grimes. **Housing for Low Income Urban Families.** Baltimore, Md: John Hopkins Press, 1976.

Halcrow Fox and Associates. **Surabaya Area Transportation Study: Summary.** London: Ministry of Overseas Development, 1977.

Jamieson MacKay and Partners. **The Minibuses and the Public Transport System of Kuala Lumpur.** Supplementary Report No. 678. Crowthorne, U.K.: TRRL, 1981.

Japan International Cooperation Agency (JICA). **Feasibility study on the second stage Expressway System in Greater Bangkok, Interim Report, Appendix, December 82.** Bangkok: Govt. of the Kingdom of Thailand, Ministry of the Interior, Expressway & Rapid Transit Authority of Thailand and the Japan International Cooperation Agency, 1982.

Japan Overseas Technical Cooperation Agency (Japan OTCA). **Urban Transport Study in Metro Manila Area.** Tokyo, 1973.

Jones, J.H., et al. **The Effects of Urban Traffic Control in Bangkok.** Supplementary Report No. 756. Crowthorne, U.K.: TRRL, 1982.

Kartodirajo, Sartano. **The Pedicab in Yogyakarta.** Jogjakarta, Indonesia: Gadjah Mada University Press, 1981.

Lim Leong Geok. **Case Study Report on Singapore.** Paris: OECD, 1975.

Linn, Johannes. **Policies for Efficient and Equitable Growth of Cities in Developing Countries.** Staff Working Paper #342. Washington, D.C.: World Bank, 1979.

_____. **Cities in the Developing World.** New York: Oxford University Press, 1983.

Little, Arthur D., et al. **Southeast Asian Regional Transport Survey.** 5 vols. Manila: Asian Development Bank, 1972.

Luna, Telesforo, et al. **The Jeepney: A Low Cost Transport Mode in Metro Manila.** Manila: Pamantasan Ng Lungsod Ng Maynila, 1978.

Mahayni, Riad G. **Transportation Planning in Third World Countries: An Annotated Bibliography.** Council of Planning Librarians, Exchange Bibliography No. 1108, 1976.

Marler, N.W. **The Performance of High-flow Bus Lanes in Bangkok.** Supplementary Report No. 723. Crowthorne, U.K.: TRRL, 1982.

Meier, A. **Intermediate Transport in South East Asia.** New York: Brookhaven National Laboratory, 1977.

Ministry of Law and National Development, Singapore. **Singapore Mass Rapid Transit Study.** Singapore, 1969.

Moohtadi, M. **Some Major Problems in the Field of Urban Transport in the City of Surabaya.** Bangkok: ECAFE Workshop on Urban Traffic and Transportation, 1971.

Ocampo, Romeo B. **Low Cost Transport in Asia.** Ottawa: International Development and Research Centre (IDRC), 1982a.

_____. **Rural Transport in the Philippines: Jeepneys, Trimobiles and Other Simple Modes in Two Bicol Towns.** Geneva: ILO, 1982b.

Organization for Economic Co-operation and Development (OECD). **The Urban Transportation Planning Process.** Paris, 1971.

_____. **Better Towns with Less Traffic.** Paris, 1975.

_____. **Paratransit in the Developing World: Neglected Options for Mobility and Employment.** 2 vols. Paris: OECD, Economic Development Centre, 1977.

_____. **Energy Problems and Urban and Suburban Transport.** Paris: OECD, Road Research Group, 1978.

_____. **Managing Transport.** Paris, 1979.

Owen, Wilfred. **Alternative Approaches to Reducing Congestion - The Case of Singapore.** Washington, D.C.: The Brookings Institute, 1972.

_____. **Automobiles and Cities, Strategies for Developing Countries.** Paris: OECD Environment Directorate, 1973.

Pendakur, V.S. **The Jeepney Driver of Manila: The Man in the Middle.** Manila: Ateneo de Manila University, 1976.

Pickup, L. and S.W. Town. **The Role of Social Science Methodologies in Transport Planning.** Supplementary Report No. 698. Crowthorne U.K.: TRRL, 1980.

Republic of Indonesia. **Jakarta Metropolitan Area Transportation**

Study. Jakarta: Directora Tata Kota Don Dacra, 1975.

_____. **Monograph on Jakarta: Development of Human Settlements in Jakarta.** Jakarta: DKI Jakarta City Administration, 1982. Prepared for the Regional Congress of Local Authorities for Development of Human Settlements, Yokohama, 9-16 June 1982; and Bangkok: ESCAP, Human Settlements Division.

Republic of the Philippines. **Metro Manila Urban Transportation Strategy Planning Project.** Part A. Inception Report. Manila: Ministry of Transportation and Communications, 1982.

_____. **Local Authorities and Human Settlements in Manila.** Paper prepared by the city of Manila for the Regional Congress of Local Authorities for Development of Human Settlements, 9-16 June 1982, Yokohama, Japan. Bangkok: ESCAP, 1982b; and Manila: Office of the City Engineer.

Rimmer, Peter. "The Future of Trishaw Enterprises in Penang". In **Food, Shelter and Transport in South East Asia and the Pacific.** Canberra: Australian National University, 1978.

Rimmer, Peter; D.W. Drakis-Smith; and T.G. McGee. **Food, Shelter, and Transport in South East Asia and the Pacific.** Canberra: Research School of Pacific Studies, Australian National University, 1978.

Roth, Gabriel. **Improving the Mobility of the Urban Poor.** Washington, D.C.: Urban Projects Dept., World Bank, 1977.

Roth, Gabriel, and George Wynn. **Free Enterprise Urban Transportation.** Washington, D.C.: Council for International Urban Liaison, 1982.

Sagasti, Francisco. **Technology, Planning and Self-reliant Development.** Toronto: Praeger Publishers, 1979.

Salih, K. **Urban Dilemmas in South East Asia.** Paper presented at the Pacific Science Association Intercongress, Singapore, September 1981. Penang: University Sains Malaysia, School of Social Sciences, 1981.

Smith, John D. **Transport Technology and Employment in Rural Malaysia.** WEP2-22/WP88. Geneva: ILO, 1981a.

_____. **Transport Technology and Employment in Rural Malaysia.** Geneva: ILO, 1981b.

Soegijoko, Budhy T.S. "Traditional Low Cost Transportation in Indonesia: The Becak; Case Study - Bandung". Mimeographed. Ottawa: International Development Research Centre, 1979.

Stringer, Peter, ed. **Transportation Planning for a Better Environment.** Paris: NATO/OECD, 1976.

Suntaranont, Tepparasit. "Social and Economic Aspects of Minibuses in Chiangmai, Thailand". Master's degree thesis. Bangkok: Asian Institute of Technology, April 1982.

Suwartoe. **Urban Traffic and Transport Problems in Djakarta.** Bangkok: ECAFE, Workshop on Urban Traffic and Transportation, 1970.

U.N. Economic and Social Commission for Asia and the Pacific (ESCAP). **Transportation For Urban and Rural Areas With Emphasis on Groups with Limited Resources.** Report prepared for UNCHS, Fifth Session, Nairobi, April-May 1982. ESCAP/G/III/7/1982. Bangkok, 1982.

U.N. Habitat. **Transportation for the Urban and Rural Areas with Emphasis on Groups with Limited Resources.** Report of the Executive Director, HC/C/5/4. Nairobi: U.N. Commission on Human Settlements, 8 February 1982.

U.N. Secretariat. **Trends and Prospects in the Population of Agglomerations, 1980-2000, As Assessed in 1973-75.** New York: United Nations, Dept. of Economic and Social Affairs, 1980.

Virabalin, Chalitpakorn, and Suchat Prasith-rathasint. **Local Authorities and Human Settlements in Bangkok.** A City Monograph prepared for the Regional Congress of Local Authorities for Development of Human Settlements, Yokohama, 9-16 June 1982. Bangkok: ESCAP, 1982.

World Bank. **Transport Sector Working Paper; Urbanization Sector Working Paper.** Washington, D.C., 1972.

_____. **Urban Transport: Sector Policy Paper.** Washington, D.C., 1975.

_____. **World Tables 1976.** Washington, D.C., 1979.

_____. **Urban Transport Sector Paper, Draft.** Washington, D.C., 1981.

_____. **World Development Report.** Washington, D.C., 1982.

World Bank. "Urban Sector Survey for Manila. Preliminary Report". Mimeographed. Washington, D.C.: Urban and Regional Economics Dept., 1975.

Zahavi, Y. **Travel Characteristics in Cities of Developing Countries.** Staff Working Paper No. 230. Washington, D.C., World Bank, 1976.

Journal Articles and Conference Papers

Ajgaonkar, R. "Transportation Planning for a New City in a Developing Country". **Transportation Planning and Technology** 2 (1974): 263-70.

Allport, R. "Improving Road-Based Public Transport in Metro Manila". Paper presented at the South-East Asia Regional Conference on Appropriate Urban Transport Technology, Manila, December 1976. Manila: Ministry of Transportation and Communications, 1976.

Chivakul, K. **Regional Growth Center: A Case Study of Chiangmai City, Thailand.** Paper presented at the International Symposium on Small Towns in National Development. Bangkok: Asian Institute of Technology, 1982.

Dent, D.M. "The Public Transport Scene in Metro Manila". **Queensland Division Technical Papers.** Brisbane, Australia: Institution of Engineers, June 1981.

Dick, H.W. "Urban Public Transport: Jakarta, Surabaya and Malang. Part I". **Bulletin of Indonesia Economic Studies** 17, no. 1 (1981a): 66-82.

_____. "Urban Public Transport: Jakarta, Surabaya and Malang. Part II". **Bulletin of Indonesia Economic Studies** 17, no. 2 (1981b): 72-89.

Financial Post. "Transportation - Malaysia, How to Get Around". Vol. 69 (12 April 1975): 13.

Goldsack, Paul J. "Metro Bonanza Brewing in Singapore". **Mass Transit** 8, no. 1 (January 1981): 54-55.

Grava, Sigurd. "The Jeepneys of Manila". **Traffic Quarterly** (October 1972): 465-83.

_____. "Paratransit in Developing Countries". In **Transportation** and **Development Around the Pacific:** **Broadening Horizons.** Proceedings of the American Society of Civil Engineers, Specialty Conference, Honolulu, 21-23 July 1980.

International Railway Journal. "Creating a Mass Transit System for Jakarta". November 1978, pp. 66-67.

Jacobs et al. "Transport Problems of the Urban Poor in Developing Countries". Paper presented at the World Conference on Transport Research, London. Crowthorne U.K.: TRRL, 1980.

Jacobs, G., and P. Fouracre. "Urban Transport in Development Countries". **Traffic Engineering and Control** (London), December 1974.

Krynetr, Prachod. "Public Transport in Bangkok". **Transports** 262 (April-May 1981).

Latchford, J.C.R. **Traffic Management in South East Asia.** Papers presented at a Conference sponsored by Hongkong Institution of Engineers and British Overseas Trade Board, Hongkong, 15-19 February 1982. London: Thomas Telford Ltd., 1982.

Leinbach, Thomas R. "The Spread of Transportation and Its Impact Upon the Modernization of Malaya, 1887-1911". **Journal of Tropical Geography** 39 (December 1974): 54-62.

_____. "Transportation and Development of Malaya". **Annals of the Association of American Geographers** 65, no. 2 (June 1975): 270-82.

tropolis. "Note sur les transport Urbains a Hong Kong". **Metropolis.** December 1976.

ierr, Jaime U. "Improving Mass Transportation in Metropolitan Manila: Some Short-range Non-capital Intensive Techniques". **Philippine Planning A Journal** 10 (April 1979): 1-24.

Overton, D.T., and J.S. Walker. "Implementing Area Traffic Control in Developing Countries". **Traffic Engineering and Control** 22, No. 5 (May 1981): 298-301.

Pendakur, V.S. "Transport Modernisation, Technology Transfer and Development Policy". Paper presented at the Congress of the Canadian Asian Studies Association, Halifax, N.S. Vancouver, B.C. The University of British Columbia, 1981a.

_____. "For A Common Cause with the Third World: Technology Transfer Issues". Paper presented at the Conference on

International Strategy: Key to Canada's Development. Victoria, B.C., Vancouver, B.C.: The University of British Columbia, 1981b.

Regulation. "Taxis, Jitneys and Mass Transit". January-February 1978, pp. 6-7.

Ridley, Tony M. "Mass Transportation in Asia". **UITP Revue** 30, no. 3 (1981): 161-72.

Rimmer, P.J. "Theories and Techniques in Third World Settings: Trishaw Peddlars and Towkays in Georgetown, Malaysia". **Australian Geographer** 15 (1982): 147-59.

Rimmer, P.J., and H.W. Dick. "Improving Urban Public Transport in Southeast Asian Cities: Some Reflections on the Conventional and Unconventional Wisdom". **Transport Policy and Decision Making** 1, no. 2/3 (1980): 97-120.

Roth, Gabriel. "Urban Transport Issues: A World Bank Approach". Proceedings of a Conference on Broadening the Horizons: Transportation and Development around the Pacific, Honolulu, Hawaii, 21-23 July 1980. New York: American Society of Civil Engineers.

_____. "Free-lance Transit: What do Third World Cities Have That Ours Don't? Flexible, Low-cost Transportation: The Surprise is How They Do It". **Reason** 14 (October 1982): 35-39.

Seah Chee-Meow. "Government Policy Choices and Public Transport Operations in Singapore". **Transport Policy and Decision Making** 1, no. 2/3 (1980): 231-51.

_____. "Mass Mobility and Accessibility: Transport Planning and Traffic Management in Singapore". **Transport Policy and Decision Making** 1, no. 1 (1980): 55-71.

Silcock, David T. "Paratransit -- The Answer". **Chartered Institute of Transport Journal** 38, no. 79 (1979): 417-20.

Steward, Frances. "Technology and Employment". **World Development** 2, no. 3 (1979).

Wafa, Jafar. "Urban Transport Planning in Developing Countries". **Transport and Communications Bulletin for Asia and the Pacific** 52 (1978): 29-32. Reprinted from **Chartered Institute of Transport Journal** 38, no. 1 (May 1978).

Walters, A.A. "The Benefits of Minibuses: The Case of Kuala

Lumpur". **Journal of Transport Economics and Policy** 13, no. 3 (September 1979): 320-34.

Wheel Extended. "Aspects of Problems and Solutions in Urban Traffic in Southeast Asia: A Round Table Discussion". Vol. 8, no. 4 (Spring 1979a): 7-13.

_____. "Urban Transport in Kuala Lumpur (Malaysia)". Vol. 8, no. 4 (1979b): 32-33.

_____. "Metro-Manila Transport System (Philippines)". Vol. 8, no. 4 (1979c): 34-35.

_____. "Urban Transport in Greater Bangkok (Thailand)". Vol. 8, no. 4 (1979d): 36-37.

_____. "Transportation Development in the Jakarta Metropolitan Area, Indonesia". Vol. 8, no. 4 (1979e): 38-40.

THE AUTHOR

Dr V. Setty Pendakur is Professor of Planning at the University of British Columbia, Canada. He is the author of several research papers and monographs on urban transport with particular reference to the developing countries. Dr Pendakur has been a consultant to the U.N. system, the World Bank, the governments in South and Southeast Asia, and Canada, with regard to the development of urban public policy and urban transport.